KFK KINGFISHER KNOWLEDGE

DANGEROUS CREATURES

KFK KINGFISHER KNOWLEDGE

DANGEROUS CREATURES

Angela Wilkes

Foreword by
Steve Leonard

KINGFISHER

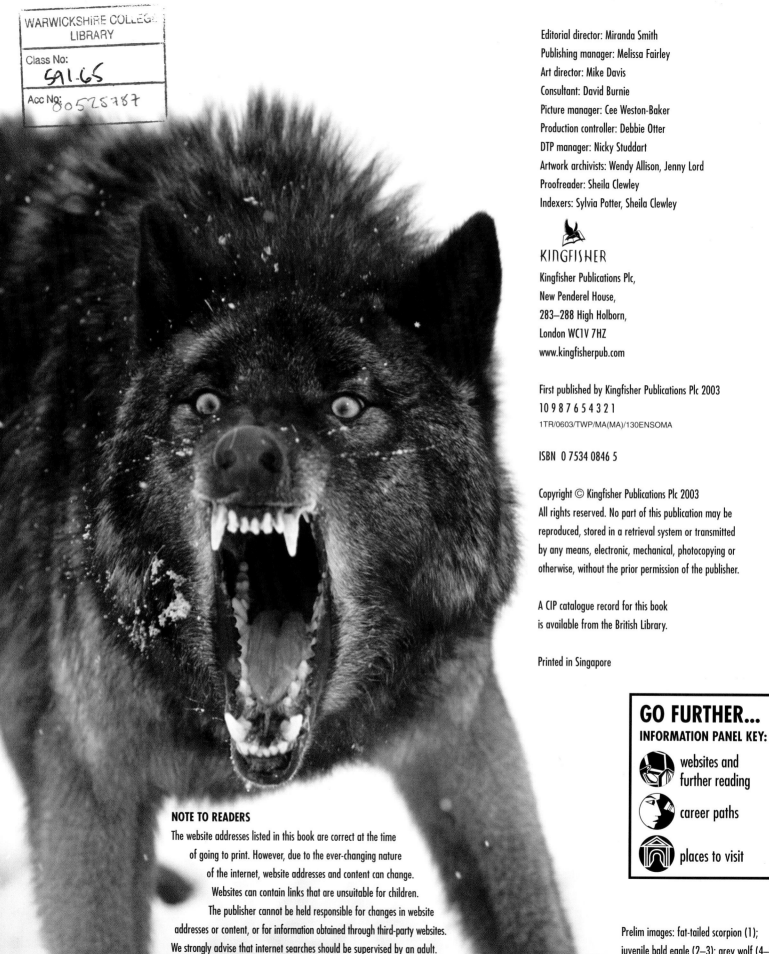

Editorial director: Miranda Smith
Publishing manager: Melissa Fairley
Art director: Mike Davis
Consultant: David Burnie
Picture manager: Cee Weston-Baker
Production controller: Debbie Otter
DTP manager: Nicky Studdart
Artwork archivists: Wendy Allison, Jenny Lord
Proofreader: Sheila Clewley
Indexers: Sylvia Potter, Sheila Clewley

KINGFISHER

Kingfisher Publications Plc,
New Penderel House,
283–288 High Holborn,
London WC1V 7HZ
www.kingfisherpub.com

First published by Kingfisher Publications Plc 2003
10 9 8 7 6 5 4 3 2 1
1TR/0603/TWP/MA(MA)/130ENSOMA

ISBN 0 7534 0846 5

A CIP catalogue record for this book
is available from the British Library.

Printed in Singapore

NOTE TO READERS

The website addresses listed in this book are correct at the time
of going to print. However, due to the ever-changing nature
of the internet, website addresses and content can change.
Websites can contain links that are unsuitable for children.
The publisher cannot be held responsible for changes in website
addresses or content, or for information obtained through third-party websites.
We strongly advise that internet searches should be supervised by an adult.

GO FURTHER...
INFORMATION PANEL KEY:

websites and
further reading

career paths

places to visit

Prelim images: fat-tailed scorpion (1);
juvenile bald eagle (2–3); grey wolf (4–5)

Contents

Foreword

Working as a vet, I have come up against animals such as large aggressive dogs and the odd crazy cat, but they were nothing compared to the dangerous creatures I met while filming around the world: lions, Komodo dragons, poisonous snakes and many more. But are these animals as deadly as we all think they are? Well... yes and no. In the right circumstances you can get quite close to many dangerous creatures with very little chance of getting hurt. I have picked up scorpions with their toxic sting and not been injured because I was shown how to handle them properly. There are lots of ways of handling poisonous snakes so as not to get bitten, but the best way is not to pick them up at all! Most animals are aggressive towards humans only when threatened.

Some animals are dangerous because they see humans as food. Creatures such as lions, crocodiles and big snakes kill and eat thousands of people around the world every year. If an animal becomes too dangerous then it has to be moved or killed. With more and more people on the planet there is less space for these animals. Magnificent beasts such as tigers are being forced into even smaller areas so they will not be a threat to the human population.

Sometimes accidents happen. I have certainly had a few! The worst was while filming sharks in South Africa. Many people are frightened by sharks, but they are not as terrifying as people think. They may look like vicious man-eaters but they rarely attack humans. Sharks have an excellent sense of smell to help them find prey, and also to taste their food before they devour it. I was diving in the sea surrounded by lots of little sharks which were looking for something to eat. One decided to have a little nibble on my leg to see if I was worth eating. Sharks' teeth are very sharp so it had no trouble biting through my wetsuit. It was busy chewing on my leg when I spun around and punched it on the nose. The shark swam away. It was not trying to eat me – my leg would have disappeared very quickly if that was the case – but just find out what I was. It was all over so quickly that I did not have time to feel really frightened.

Working with dangerous creatures has taught me to respect them and try to understand them more. I feel very privileged to have entered their world, and I want others to understand that these creatures need protection from humans much more than we need protection from them.

Steve Leonard – veterinary surgeon, and presenter of the BBC's *Ultimate Killers*

CHAPTER 1

Tooth and claw

Predators have to kill other animals in order to eat. Many of them will also attack or kill other animals in self-defence, or to defend their young or their home territory. In order to hunt successfully, predators have super-sharp senses. Keen eyesight, an acute sense of smell and an excellent sense of hearing enable them to track down their prey. But equally important are a predator's body weapons, the fearsome tools it uses to catch and kill its prey.

Large carnivores, such as bears, big cats, wolves, sharks, birds of prey and crocodiles all have a formidable battery of physical weapons. Razor-sharp teeth, dagger-like claws and ferocious beaks equip them to tackle animals almost as big as themselves. These predators are not only strong, they can often move at great speed, or use stealth to track down their prey. This makes them very dangerous to humans.

grizzly bear

Deadly weapons

All predators, whatever type of animal they are, need fierce and powerful weapons with which to catch and kill their prey. Large predators, such as the big cats and eagles, hunt big, fast-moving animals. It is vital that they are able to bring their prey down and kill it swiftly, before it has a chance to escape.

Each of these efficient predators has evolved its own highly specialized set of body weapons, which may be ferocious fangs, long, hooked claws or a fierce beak. These lethal weapons are pointed and razor-sharp, and are used for the initial kill as well as for tearing apart the prey's flesh afterwards.

▲ Eagles and other birds of prey kill animals with the long, curved claws called talons at the tips of their toes. They attack their prey feet first, swinging the talons forwards as they swoop from the skies. The victim is caught in a vice-like grip by both the toes and talons, and is either crushed so it cannot breathe, or stabbed to death with the dagger-like back talons.

▶ Big cats, such as this lioness, are armed with powerful jaws and fierce teeth. Cats clamp their teeth around the neck or throat of their prey to suffocate it. The cat's long, fang-like canine teeth stab, rip and tear through their victim's flesh. The smaller teeth at the front of the mouth nibble off meat, and the large, sharp teeth at the back of the mouth can slice through tough gristle and crack bones.

Built for speed
The cheetah hunts fast-moving prey such as gazelle, which live in open grassland. It does not pounce on its quarry, but stalks it, keeping as low to the ground as possible, then sprints forwards and gives chase. A cheetah can cover 7m in a single bound and maintain a speed of 70km/h for several kilometres, swerving this way and that as the prey tries to throw it off. It can reach an astounding top speed of 113km/h, but it can only keep this up for a few 100m before its energy runs out.

▲ The largest and heaviest of all the big cats, the tiger is a night hunter. It tracks down animals smaller than itself, such as deer and wild pigs. Tigers do not usually hunt humans, but occasionally they do become man-eaters.

Stealth and speed

Cats are masterly hunters and bring down their prey with a lethal combination of stealth, speed and strength. Most cats, from the tiger to the domestic tabby, are solitary hunters and operate in a similar way: they stalk their quarry, slinking forwards slowly and silently, then rush ahead and pounce, sinking their teeth into the prey's neck. Even the heaviest cats, such as tigers and lions, can leap with great power and agility.

The cheetah, however, is different. This cat runs rather than leaps, and has developed the body of a true sprinter, making it the fastest animal on land in the world.

Long tail held out behind the cheetah helps it keep its balance

▶ Unlike the other big cats, the cheetah has narrow, dog-like paws with special paw pads to help it run fast. Its non-retractable claws help the cheetah to keep a good grip on the ground as it sprints along.

The cheetah is smaller and slimmer than all the other big cats. It has a strong but lightweight skeleton with long, slim legs. The extended, flexible spine works like a spring, powering its huge leaps across the ground and enabling it to turn and swerve to keep up with its quarry. The cheetah's skull is small and light and its eyes are spaced far apart, so that it can focus on its prey's movements. Unlike other cats, cheetahs do not have sheaths over their claws and cannot retract them. Like running spikes, they give the cheetah a good grip on the ground. Its long tail acts as a rudder, helping it to keep balanced while it twists and turns.

Stealthy hunters

The other big cats cannot run fast over any great distance, so they rely on stealth rather than speed to catch their prey. They stalk the target as closely as possible before breaking cover, then spring for the kill. This demands both strength and agility, as the cat usually pounces onto its prey's back before sinking its teeth in. Most of the big cats hunt animals that are smaller than they are, because they hunt alone. The only exceptions to this rule are lionesses. They hunt in a family group, so can bring down larger prey which they share among the pride.

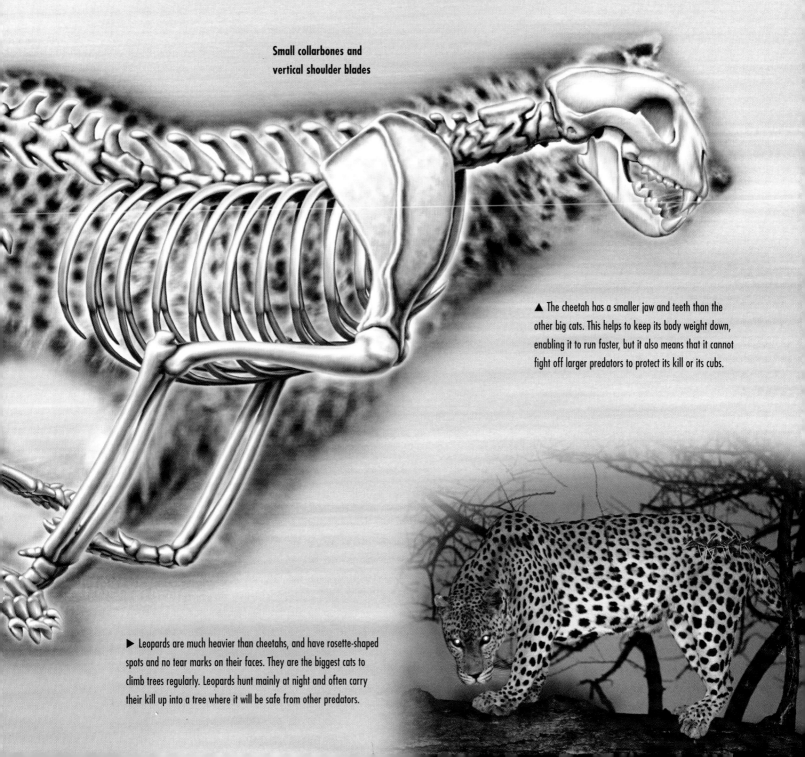

Small collarbones and vertical shoulder blades

▲ The cheetah has a smaller jaw and teeth than the other big cats. This helps to keep its body weight down, enabling it to run faster, but it also means that it cannot fight off larger predators to protect its kill or its cubs.

▶ Leopards are much heavier than cheetahs, and have rosette-shaped spots and no tear marks on their faces. They are the biggest cats to climb trees regularly. Leopards hunt mainly at night and often carry their kill up into a tree where it will be safe from other predators.

◀ A hungry polar bear tears at a seal carcass on the sea ice. When food is plentiful, experienced polar bears eat only the seal's blubber and skin, leaving the flesh. Younger bears and arctic foxes will finish off the grisly remains of the carcass.

Mighty carnivores

Polar bears weigh up to 600kg and are the largest land predators in the world. Not only are they huge, but they are also powerful swimmers, and can run faster than reindeer over short distances.

Polar bears roam the sea-ice along the coastlines that border the Arctic Ocean. They hunt mainly seals, not only on the ice but in the water, where they also attack walruses and beluga whales. Seals swim below the ice, but come up for air at breathing holes. A polar bear will lie in wait by a breathing hole, attacking a seal when it comes to the surface.

Death blow

The polar bear kills a seal with a mighty swipe of one of its massive front paws. Then it hauls the seal out of the hole, and rips it apart with sharp teeth. If a polar bear sniffs out a seal's birthing den hidden beneath the ice, it rears up on its back legs, then drops on all fours down onto the roof of the den, to smash through the sea-ice and reach the baby seals below.

Massive strength

Despite their lovable image, bears are savage predators. They hunt alone and rely on their enormous strength to catch and kill large animals. A bear's strength comes from its size, weight and sheer muscle-power. As a rule, bears avoid contact with people, but they are very dangerous if taken by surprise, particularly when with cubs or feeding from a kill. But bears are not the only large animals to fear. Giant plant-eaters, such as elephants and hippopotamuses, are also strong because of their size, and can be highly dangerous if they feel threatened.

◀ A charging elephant can run at speeds of up to 40km/h. It is also strong enough to knock down any trees in its way.

A grizzly bear usually only rears to its full height of over 2m because it is curious about something and wants to have a good look around. A show of aggression, however, means that the bear has been taken by surprise and is probably very frightened.

A grizzly end

The grizzly bear is regarded as one of the most dangerous animals in North America. It is big enough to kill a moose, and can break the neck or back of most large animals with a blow from one of its giant paws. It can charge at speeds of up to 64km/h and is an excellent swimmer. The grizzly bear is also skilful at fishing. It stands in the shallows below waterfalls and catches salmon as they leap upstream on the way to their spawning grounds.

Giant plant-eaters

Elephants and hippopotamuses are not predators, they are plant-eaters. In Asia, however, many people are injured or killed every year by elephants raiding farmland to feed on crops. Bull elephants, particularly Asian ones, also have periods of aggressive behaviour called 'musth', during which they try to establish dominance over their rivals. At times like these, they can be unpredictable and dangerous.

In Africa, the hippopotamus causes more deaths each year than any other large animal, including the big cats. In rivers such as the Nile, male hippopotamuses have areas called territories which they guard fiercely. They are very aggressive towards each other, and will attack small boats that invade their territories.

Teamwork

Some predators hunt in teams, even though they are quite capable of catching prey on their own. A team has a higher chance of a successful kill than one animal working alone, and it can bring down bigger prey. Working as a team is also safer, because it means that there are more eyes watching out for other dangerous predators. Each member of the team may end up with a little less food once the spoils of the kill are shared out, but hunting in this way ensures that the group as a whole is more likely to survive.

▼ An African buffalo is too large and dangerous for a lioness to tackle on her own. Four lionesses have chased this buffalo into a deep swamp from which it cannot escape, and are moving in for the kill.

▲ African hunting dogs are thin and lightly built, but have enormous stamina. This means that they are able to pursue prey over long distances.

Stalking tactics

Lionesses work in small groups to hunt large prey, such as wildebeest and zebra. When approaching a herd, they spread out in a line and move forwards slowly, stalking, then freeze, crouching. When they are within 20m of the herd, they single out a victim and give chase. One lioness leaps onto the prey and the others close in quickly.

Family packs

African wild dogs are perhaps the most efficient team hunters of all. They can bring down the largest prey in relation to their body size, and four out of every five hunts are successful. The dogs live in tightly-knit family packs of up to 20 adults and their pups. They hunt together and share every catch with the whole pack, including the young.

The hunting party sets off at dusk. African wild dogs hunt gazelle and antelope, but sometimes wildebeest and zebra too. They pinpoint a weak animal, then form a semi-circle and chase it relentlessly. They can run at a steady speed of 40km/h for up to 5km, and they harry their prey by taking it in turns to snap at its sides and rear. When the prey gets tired, the dogs drag it down with their teeth and tear it apart.

A pack of wolves can bring down prey as large as a moose or bison. Up to 30 wolves make up a family group, which patrols and defends its own hunting territory. Wolves hunt mainly caribou and other deer. When they have found a herd, they dart at the animals to find out which ones are old or weak, before giving chase. Sometimes they circle the prey and then close in. At other times they run the prey down, or one group drives it into an ambush set up by the rest of the pack.

▶ Wolves share the kill out among the entire pack. The first share goes to the leaders of the pack – the alpha male and alpha female – and the senior hunters. Less active members of the pack and the young cubs have to wait until last.

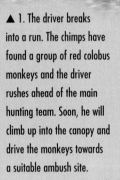

Killer chimps

Deep in the rainforests of West Africa, chimpanzees often group together to form teams of savage hunters. Their favourite prey are red colobus monkeys, and they hunt them down with ruthless cunning and skill. Each of the chimps has a specific role to play in a complex hunting strategy, either as a driver, a blocker, an ambusher or a chaser.

▲ 1. The driver breaks into a run. The chimps have found a group of red colobus monkeys and the driver rushes ahead of the main hunting team. Soon, he will climb up into the canopy and drive the monkeys towards a suitable ambush site.

▲ 2. A blocker takes up his position in a tree. His job is to cut off the monkeys' escape route. He makes sure that he is sitting in full view of the fleeing monkeys, then bares his teeth fiercely and screams loudly. This frightens the monkeys and sends them running straight ahead towards the final trap.

2. Blocker

4. Ambusher

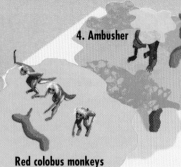

Red colobus monkeys

2. Blocker

3. Chasers

1. Driver

▶ This scene shows the chimpanzees' hunting strategy. Each member of the hunting team is in position, and the chasers are closing in for the kill. The red arrow indicates the direction of the chase.

▶ 3. Three chasers hoot and screech loudly as they wait to join the chase. They are strong young males and it is their job to keep the red colobus monkeys moving through the trees towards the ambusher, and to catch them if they can.

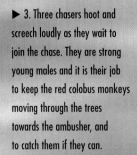

The chase

The hunt begins when one of the chimps, the driver, springs up a tree to separate some of the monkeys from their group. He then drives them towards the place where the other chimps are setting up their ambush. The blockers climb into the trees on either side of the ambush site and make sure they are easily visible. The ambusher rushes ahead and finds a place to hide. Now the chasers join in. They leap up into the trees after the monkeys and chase them towards the ambusher's hiding-place.

▶ 4. The ambusher, usually the oldest and most experienced member of the hunting team, waits silently and concentrates on the chase from his hiding-place among the leaves.

The kill

Now it is time for the ambusher to join the action. With the chasers hot on their heels, and the blockers to the sides, the desperate red colobus monkeys are heading right into his trap. At exactly the right moment, the ambusher jumps up in front of them and the panic-stricken monkeys have nowhere to turn.

Sharing the spoils

The chimps either tear the monkeys apart up in the trees or carry them down to the ground, where the rest of their group are hooting with excitement. The senior members of the group take most of the meat, but if there is enough to go around, other chimps also get a share. Then, quiet at last, but with bloodied hands and faces, the chimpanzees gnaw and chew on their spoils.

Danger from the skies

For small animals, danger can come literally out of the blue. Not only are they hunted by predators on the ground; a threat can also come from the skies. Birds that hunt other animals are called birds of prey. They are also known as raptors, from the Latin word 'rapere', meaning 'to seize'. Eagles, falcons and hawks are birds of prey that hunt by day. Owls, on the other hand, hunt by night.

All predators need special equipment in order to hunt successfully. Birds of prey have highly developed senses to help them locate their victims, powerful wings for giving chase and razor-sharp talons and beaks for executing the kill.

▲ A Harris hawk, a bird of prey from the American deserts, prepares to swoop. The wings and tail are fanned out to hold the bird steady while it lines up its prey for an attack.

Night hunters

As night falls, owls set off to hunt. Some fly low over the countryside, looking for prey, but others settle on a high vantage point, such as a tree or rock. Owls have enormous eyes that are specially adapted to see in the dark. They also have an acute sense of hearing and can pinpoint the sound of an animal moving in total darkness, provided there is very little background noise.

Once it has located a mouse or some other small animal, the owl swoops in for the kill. The prey rarely hears it coming. Owls can fly silently, as their primary flight feathers have fringed edges which muffle the sound of air passing through them. The owl seizes the prey, then flies back to its perch to eat.

Hunting on the wing

Each bird of prey has its own hunting technique. Most of them soar high in the skies, scouring the ground for signs of movement. A bird of prey's eyesight is about eight times sharper than a human's, and a bird such as a buzzard can spot, from the sky, a rabbit over 3km away.

Some raptors, such as the peregrine falcon, dive down from the sky to catch their prey, reaching speeds of up to 200km/h. Others, such as the golden eagle, flush out their quarry. It soars in the sky until it spots a rabbit or small animal, then flaps away, loses height and flies in low from one side, taking its victim by surprise. All birds of prey catch and kill their prey with their deadly talons, swinging them forwards just before the attack.

◀ Highly focused, and with its legs and talons outstretched, a tawny owl drops down upon an unsuspecting field mouse. The owl holds its wings back to act as brakes as it comes in for the kill.

The kill
Many birds of prey carry their catch back to their roost or a favourite plucking post before eating it. Falcons, hawks and eagles do not swallow their prey whole, as it is usually far too big. Instead, they hold their food down with both feet while they tear it apart. A bird of prey's sharp, hooked bill is not generally used for killing prey, but it is the perfect shape for tearing off limbs and ripping off strips of flesh. It works rather like a combination of a butcher's knife and a meat hook.

Most birds just rip the meat and entrails from their catch, discarding any bones and fur. They usually pluck the feathers, as they cannot digest them. The ground beneath a bird of prey's plucking post is often strewn with feathers.

Owls are the only birds of prey that swallow their prey whole. After they have eaten their catch, they sit very still while they digest the meal. Inside a part of the owl's gut called the gizzard, the meat is separated from the prey's fur and bones, which the owl cannot digest. These are formed into sausage-like pellets which the owl coughs up once or twice a day. Pulling an owl pellet apart is a good way to discover just what the owl ate for its last meal.

▲ The Harris hawk is one of the few birds of prey that hunts in groups. Three or four birds gather on nearby perches and take it in turns to fly high and survey the surrounding countryside for prey. They then harass their victim or surprise it with an ambush.

▼ The peregrine falcon catches ducks and other birds, which it devours at its favourite plucking post. It starts eating the prey at the neck, after pulling out a few feathers, and often removes the bird's head and wings.

Danger in the water

Crocodiles and their relatives – alligators, gharials and caimans – are the largest living reptiles on earth, and they are fierce predators. They lurk unseen in rivers, lakes and swamps in hot, tropical countries, lying in wait for prey. Saltwater crocodiles, the biggest of all, live in the brackish water of river estuaries, or in the sea.

Crocodiles' huge, scaly bodies, giant jaws and crooked teeth give them a prehistoric look, and indeed their ancestors date back 200 million years, to the time of the dinosaurs. The crocodiles' unique hunting skills have made them efficient predators and extraordinary survivors.

▲ Although almost 7m long, this saltwater crocodile has made itself nearly invisible to any nearby animals. It is lying almost completely submerged in the water, with only its eyes, its ears and some of the scales on its back clearly visible.

Ambush and attack

Crocodiles and alligators eat a wide range of prey, from fish and birds to large mammals, such as zebra and wildebeest. They rarely attack and kill humans, but may do so if they feel that their territory is being invaded.

Most crocodiles lie in ambush, as this saves energy, and float near the shore of a river or lake, waiting for animals to come down to the water to drink. As they lie partly submerged in the water, they are completely camouflaged and can breathe, smell and hear without being seen.

▼ A herd of wildebeest is drinking at the river, when suddenly an enormous Nile crocodile lunges out of the water and grabs the nearest animal in its jaws. Unable to tear itself free, the wildebeest is dragged into the water.

► An American alligator basks in the sun on a sandbank. It opens its mouth to help it keep cool, showing a frightening array of teeth.

Ripped into bite-sized chunks!

As soon as an animal comes too close, a crocodile attacks. It shoots forwards out of the water, clamps its jaws around the animal's leg or muzzle, and pulls it into deeper water to drown it. It drags the animal underwater, then rolls over and over, like a spinning top, to rip it apart. Large prey often die from a broken spine as they are spun in the water. Crocodiles have to do this, as their jaws are not strong enough to tear off pieces of flesh, and they are not able to chew. Their prey has to be gradually ripped into bite-sized chunks that they can then swallow whole.

Weapons and armoury

Crocodiles have two to three times as many teeth as humans – a Nile crocodile has 68 teeth and an American alligator has 80 – but they are short and cone-shaped, rather than being particularly sharp. A crocodile constantly grows new teeth, so if one tooth wears out or falls out, another one grows to take its place.

Despite their bulky appearance, crocodiles and alligators are fast and agile. Powerful tails propel them through the water and give them a burst of power as they surge ashore. Their leathery skin is reinforced with bony plates called scutes, making it as tough as armour-plating.

A crocodile's ears and nostrils close underwater and a third eyelid closes across its eyes to protect them. Flaps at the back of the crocodile's throat stop water entering its lungs when it opens its mouth underwater to tear prey apart.

◀ A young Cape fur seal is flung
2m up into the air after a glancing
blow from the shark's massive jaw.

▼ A great white shark breaches, leaping straight out of the sea
in pursuit of a seal. Young seals are most at risk — more than
80 per cent of all shark attacks are on young or baby seals.

Ocean hunters

The most feared creatures of the
oceans are the big sharks and
toothed whales. Sharks have a chilling
reputation because of their speed in the
water, their terrifying teeth and their ability to
sense any blood in the sea from a great distance.
Some sharks, such as the great white, have been known
to attack people, but they usually do this because they
mistake them for prey. A big shark hunts fish, seals and sea lions.

▼ A killer whale surfs onto a beach to grab
a sea lion, before turning on its flank
and heading back out to sea.

Ocean giants

Killer whales are the largest predators among the
warm-blooded mammals of the world. They were given
their name not because they attack people, but because
they have been known to kill other whales. They can grow
to more than 6m in length, and have streamlined bodies
with striking black and white markings. Killer whales
hunt seals, sea lions, penguins and walruses. Some
specialize in sliding out onto sand bars or ice floes
to catch prey, and have even been known to
bump the ice floes from below to knock their
victims into the sea. Like wolves and lionesses,
killer whales often hunt together, in groups
called pods. They round up their prey and
herd it into a small area before attacking.

Efficient hunter

The great white shark is considered by many to be the most frightening creature in the sea. Measuring up to 6m in length, it has a sleek torpedo-shaped body and a powerful, crescent-shaped tail which propels it through the water at great speed. Its upper jaw is armed with triangular teeth with serrated edges that can slice through flesh, blubber and bone. Its lower jaw is lined with long, pointed teeth that it uses to hold and slice through prey.

▶ Like all sharks, tiger sharks have tiny pits in their snouts. Special nerves inside them help the shark to detect electrical signals given off by the muscles of its prey.

▲ Sharks are able to locate prey because they have a whole range of highly tuned senses that help them to pick up the sounds and vibrations of other animals moving through the water. They can smell blood and other body fluids in the water from over 1km away, and the nerves in their snouts enable them to pick up tiny electrical signals given off by other animals. As the shark moves closer to a target, it can sense changes in the movement of the water which help it to home in on its prey.

In for the kill

The great white shark cruises along the sea-bed just off the coast, in search of prey such as seals and sea lions. The shark is not really white, but has a pale belly and a dark back, making it hard for prey in the water above to spot it against the ocean floor. The great white shark usually attacks from below. When it spots a seal, it shoots upwards at speeds of up to 48km/h. As it goes in for the kill, its eyes roll back and its lower jaw opens. From that moment on, it relies on the electrical sensors in its snout to pinpoint its prey with deadly accuracy.

SUMMARY OF CHAPTER 1: TOOTH AND CLAW

Tooth and claw

This chapter looked at how the large carnivores attack and kill their prey. All of these predators are armed with fierce body weapons, such as sharp teeth, powerful jaws, barbed talons or a hooked beak.

Stealth, speed and strength

The big cats use a combination of stealth, speed and strength to bring down prey. Most of them stalk their quarries and then pounce on them. The cheetah hunts fast-moving prey, so it gives chase at high speed. In fact, it is the fastest-moving animal on land. Bears rely on their size and strength to catch large animals. Polar bears hunt for seals and a grizzly bear is strong enough to catch a moose. Large plant-eaters, such as elephants, can also be aggressive and dangerous.

Teamwork

Some predators hunt in teams, giving them a greater chance of a successful kill. African hunting dogs and wolves hunt in packs, and lionesses work in small family groups to hunt large animals. Chimpanzees organize brutal hunting parties to catch and kill monkeys.

Lone hunters

Birds of prey, such as eagles, hawks and owls, patrol the skies looking out for prey. When they spot an animal, they swoop down and kill it with their outstretched talons, then tear the prey apart with their hooked beaks.

Crocodiles and alligators rely on ambush tactics. They lurk in rivers until an animal comes down to drink, then lunge forward and grab it in their powerful jaws. They usually drown an animal before eating it.

Sharks and killer whales cruise through the oceans in search of prey. Sharks are highly sensitive and can locate prey from a long way off. Sleek and powerful, they attack at great speed and clamp their massive jaws around their target, ripping through its flesh with teeth like knives.

Go further...

Learn all about animals on the BBC website: www.bbc.co.uk/reallywild

For information on British birds, including birds of prey, visit the RSPB website: www.rspb.org.uk

For information on different types of shark, and shark conservation, visit: www.sharktrust.org/

Ultimate Killers by Steve Leonard (Boxtree, 2001)

The Life of Mammals by David Attenborough (BBC Books, 2002)

The Big Cat Diary by Brian Jackman and Jonathan Scott (BBC Books, 1996)

Zoologist
Studies animals and their characteristics, and classifies them.

Primatologist
Studies apes and their conservation.

Ornithologist
Specializes in the study of birds.

Park warden/ranger
This involves looking after nature reserves. Experience as a volunteer will help you enormously.

Wildlife photographer or cameraman
Photographing or filming wildlife for books, magazines or television programmes.

Visit Whipsnade Wild Animal Park, Europe's largest wildlife conservation park, for an opportunity to see large animals in natural surroundings.
www.whipsnade.co.uk
Whipsnade Wild Animal Park,
Dunstable,
Bedfordshire, LU6 2LF
T: 01582 872 171

Monkey World Ape Rescue Centre has rescued monkeys and apes from all over the world. There are 56 chimpanzees – the largest group outside Africa.
www.monkeyworld.co.uk
Monkey World Ape Rescue Centre,
Wareham, Dorset, BH20 6HH
T: 01929 462 537

green mamba

CHAPTER 2

Venomous creatures

Some predators do not have the sheer size and strength to wrestle with their prey and bring it down. They may also not have the right body parts: snakes, for example, have no limbs with which to hang on to their victim. Instead of fighting and risking injury, these animals simply use poison. Their venom paralyzes their victims so that they cannot escape, or kills them outright. This gives the predator time to consume its meal at leisure.

Poisons are a complex mixture of different chemicals. Some animals, including many which use poison in self-defence only, have very powerful venom for their body size. Animals have different ways of injecting poison into their victims. Some have fangs; others use spines, stings or even hairs. All these devices work like hypodermic needles, injecting venom straight into the bloodstream so it takes effect quickly.

Portuguese man o'war

Venomous creatures

A huge range of animals – from snakes and spiders to giant jellyfish and tiny frogs – are poisonous. Animal poisons, often called venom or toxins, can be deadly chemical weapons. Some poisons just cause pain: others kill. Many animals use poison purely for self-defence, to protect themselves from predators. Others use it to paralyze or kill their prey – as poisons act quickly, they are a highly effective means of subduing fast-moving prey before it has a chance to escape.

Types of venom

There are two main types of venom. One affects an animal's nervous system, paralyzing the victim and leading to suffocation or a heart attack. The other stops an animal's blood system from working.

Venom is usually injected into victims by means of needle-sharp fangs, spines or stings, but it can also be in an animal's saliva, or the slimy mucus covering its skin.

Killer tentacles

Jellyfish and their relatives ensnare prey in their long, trailing tentacles. Each tentacle is covered with stinging cells. As soon as the tentacles touch prey – or a person – poisonous darts shoot out from the stinging cells. These hold, poison and paralyze the prey so the jellyfish can lift it to its mouth.

Injecting venom

Sea anemones and coral polyps catch
food in a similar way to jellyfish, but
many sea creatures use sharp spines
to inject venom into prey or predators.

Poisonous fangs

Many snakes, such as this eyelash
viper (right), are armed with poisonous
fangs. A snake's fangs are thin, sharp
and curve backwards, so it can get
a good grip on prey. Snakes strike fast,
jabbing their victims with their fangs
and injecting a strong dose of venom
into them. The venom of some
snakes is powerful enough to paralyze
and kill quite large animals. Spiders
also have a poisonous bite which
they use to paralyze or kill their prey.
    Some poisonous animals are
brightly coloured or patterned.
This warns predators that they
are dangerous and best left alone.

▲ A king cobra lunges forwards to attack, in typical threat posture with its hood on display. It can hold itself upright with up to one third of its total length – almost 2m – and move forwards with alarming speed, making a low, hissing sound rather like a dog's growl.

Feared snakes

Deadly venom, lightning speed, long, sinuous bodies and flickering, forked tongues make people fear snakes more than most other animals. Many snakes grow several metres long and can swallow extremely large prey, making them all the more daunting. Poisonous snakes do not hunt people, but use their venom to immobilize or kill the small animals that they eat, such as rats or lizards. They only bite humans to defend themselves when they feel threatened. Some snake venom is so powerful that it can kill a person unless they are treated quickly.

▼ The Gaboon viper has a huge body 2m long, and lives in the tropical rainforests of western and central Africa. It relies on camouflage to help it catch rodents and frogs. It lies in wait on the forest floor, its vivid geometric markings making it almost invisible against the surrounding leaf litter. The Gaboon viper has fangs that are 5cm long – the longest fangs of any snake.

Deadly poison

The inland taipan, the most poisonous land snake, has such strong venom that a full dose can kill a human within 45 minutes. In fact, the taipan lives only in remote parts of inland Australia, and is so rarely seen that at one time people thought it was extinct. The inland taipan's main prey are rats, which move fast and can be dangerous as they bite and scratch. It is vital for a snake to have strong venom which will immobilize the rats quickly before they can cause injury. The taipan's venom attacks an animal's nervous system, stopping it from breathing and causing paralysis.

◄ The inland taipan rears up aggressively in its characteristic 'S' shape, ready to strike, revealing its bright yellow belly. The inland taipan is not known to have caused any human deaths at all.

Giant among snakes

King cobras are the largest venomous snakes of all, and can grow up to 5.5m in length. They live in the tropical forests of Southeast Asia and eat snakes and lizards. When the king cobra feels threatened, it hisses, rears up and spreads out its neck ribs to form a hood which makes it look more frightening. One bite from a king cobra is lethal enough to kill an elephant. Indeed, up to 36 people die from king cobra bites every year.

Fastest snake

Almost 4m long, the black mamba is one of the most feared snakes in Africa. It can move faster than any other snake, slithering along the ground at speeds of up to 16km/h, with its head held high. Despite its speed, its aim is both swift and accurate.

The black mamba often lives in termite mounds or hollow trees, and hunts rodents, ground squirrels and other small mammals. Unlike other snakes, which swallow their prey alive, it bites its victims and then leaves them to die before eating them. The black mamba's venom is very strong and attacks the nervous system.

▼ The black mamba is slender but very strong. In fact, it is not black, but a metallic greyish-green colour. It may get its name from the colour inside its mouth, which is purplish-black. Just two drops of its venom can kill a person.

Poisonous fangs

All snakes are meat eaters, but they have no limbs with which to hold down prey and no teeth with which to chew it. So, many snakes are armed with lethal poisonous fangs instead. These work rather like hypodermic needles. They inject poison into prey and paralyze or kill it. This gives a snake the time to swallow its quarry whole, safe from the danger of an active victim's sharp teeth or claws.

▶ A rattlesnake opens its mouth wide to strike, then sinks its two long fangs into an animal. As it does so, venom is squeezed out of the venom glands and along tiny tubes called ducts into the snake's hollow fangs. The venom is then forced out of small openings in the fangs and injected into the deep puncture wounds that the fangs have made. It enters the victim's bloodstream instantly and is so powerful that it takes effect straight away.

Heat-seeking snakes

Pit vipers, the family of poisonous snakes that includes rattlesnakes, cottonmouths and bushmasters, have the most sophisticated fangs and detection devices of all the snakes. They have heat-sensitive pits or hollows on the sides of their faces which pick up infrared heat given off by nearby prey. This means that pit vipers can pinpoint prey in total darkness without being able to see at all. Pit vipers rely on ambush tactics to catch their quarry. They strike with lightning speed and inject their venom into their prey, then often wait for five to 30 minutes for the venom to take effect. Even if the prey manages to escape, it is too weak to go far and the snake soon tracks it down.

Poisonous cocktail

Snake venom is like saliva or spit – but with a potent mixture of deadly chemicals. Each type of poisonous snake has its own type of venom, depending on the chemicals in it. A rattlesnake's venom mainly affects a victim's blood system. A snake's venom does not just subdue or kill its prey. Like saliva, it starts to dissolve and break down the snake's food, as the first step of the digestive process. Snakes can control the amount of venom they inject, so that they do not waste any. Although they do not need to eat as often as mammals, it can take a while to replace their supply of venom. Snakes are in danger from predators during this time.

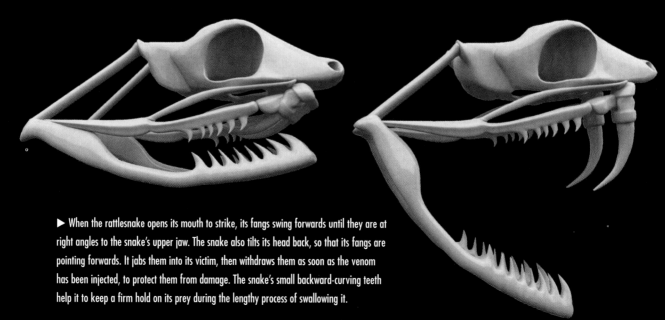

▶ Normally, a rattlesnake's long, slender fangs are folded up flat against its upper jaw on either side of its mouth. This stops them from sticking out of the snake's mouth when it is closed. The fangs are tucked into a sheath of skin, to protect them and keep their points really sharp.

▶ When the rattlesnake opens its mouth to strike, its fangs swing forwards until they are at right angles to the snake's upper jaw. The snake also tilts its head back, so that its fangs are pointing forwards. It jabs them into its victim, then withdraws them as soon as the venom has been injected, to protect them from damage. The snake's small backward-curving teeth help it to keep a firm hold on its prey during the lengthy process of swallowing it.

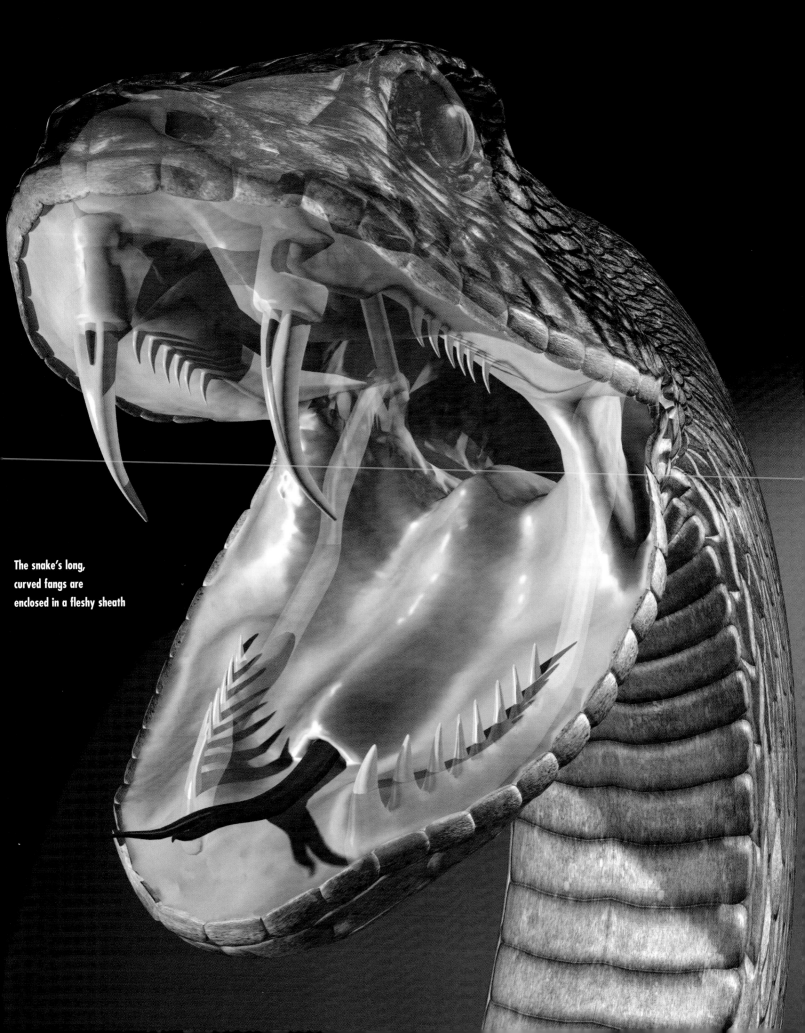

The snake's long,
curved fangs are
enclosed in a fleshy sheath

◄ The golden poison-dart frog is a close relative of the terrible frog, the most venomous frog of all. It is one of only three species of frog that are toxic enough to produce effective blow gun darts.

▼ Strawberry poison-dart frogs are named after their bright red skin speckled with blue-black markings. These two frogs are peering over the rim of a bromeliad leaf, high in the rainforest canopy.

Venomous skin

Even small, harmless-looking animals can be deadly poisonous. Amphibians, a group of animals that includes frogs, toads and salamanders, are born in water, yet live on land as adults. They all have thin, moist skin through which they breathe, and many of them have skin that is poisonous.

The poison is produced by poison glands on the amphibian's back or scattered throughout its skin. The poison tastes nasty and discourages predators from eating the amphibian. The most poisonous amphibians of all are very brightly coloured. These colours act as a warning to predators that the animal is dangerous to eat.

Colourful frogs

Poison-dart frogs, which live in the rainforests of Central and South America, secrete the most powerful skin poison of any amphibian. The poison is scattered throughout the frogs' skin and acts fast, attacking the nerve and muscle cells of a predator and causing heart failure. Poison-dart frogs are so called because the Choco tribe in South America uses their poison on the tips of their darts. One frog produces enough poison for up to 50 darts. Poison-dart frogs are tiny, only up to 5cm long, and are many jewel-like colours. These provide such an effective warning to predators that the frogs are active and can search for food by day, unlike other frogs.

The most poisonous frog of all, the terrible frog, produces up to 2g of poison, just one tenth of which could kill a man.

▲ The enormous cane toad has a large pouch-like swelling on each shoulder. These are its parotid glands (near the ears), big glands that produce toxins. More toxins are concentrated in the toad's warty skin, its muscles, bones and body organs. The toad's eggs and tadpoles are also poisonous.

Poisonous toad

All toads have slightly poisonous skin that makes predators avoid eating them. The cane toad, however, is not only very large, weighing up to 2kg, it is also very poisonous. Toxins are spread throughout its body, but are concentrated in its warty skin and the two glands on its shoulders. When a toad is attacked, milky venom from these glands oozes into its attacker's mouth, causing heart failure, convulsions, temporary blindness, and even death.

Beetle control

Originally from South and Central America, the cane toad was introduced to Australia 60 years ago, to try to control beetles infesting sugar cane crops, and soon spread rapidly. All the predators of native Australian frogs, such as water birds and snakes, die from eating the toad.

Living in fire

The fire salamander grows up to 30cm long and has a black body with yellow markings, to warn predators that it is poisonous. Its skin produces toxins that taste nasty, irritate the eyes and can even kill small mammals. The salamander also has poison glands on its back and squirts poison in the face of persistent predators. The word salamander means 'lives in fire'. People used to think salamanders could survive fire, because they ran out of logs on campfires when they were lit.

▼ The black and yellow skin markings of the fire salamander are characteristic warning colours. Other colour combinations that work in the same way are red and black, and orange and black.

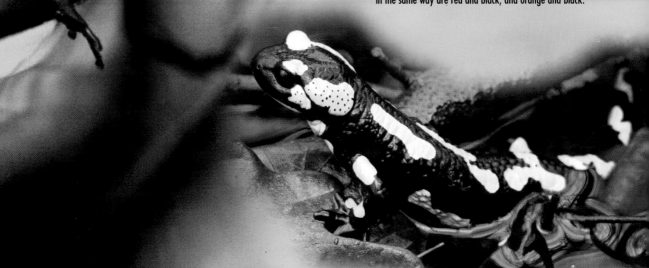

forked tongue

A deadly bite

Two completely contrasting kinds of lizard, living in two different parts of the world, have an especially nasty bite. They do not just use their sharp teeth to kill their prey: one has a poisonous bite and the other has a mouth full of deadly bacteria. The Gila monster is a brightly coloured lizard found in the southwestern United States. The Komodo dragon, a monitor lizard, lives on only a handful of small, isolated islands in Indonesia, and is known locally as an 'ora'.

▲ The Gila monster has bead-like scaly skin that is black with pink and yellow markings. It has dark bands on its tail, a black face and black legs and feet. Its bright colours probably warn predators that it is poisonous.

Venomous lizard

The Gila monster is one of only two poisonous lizards and grows up to 50cm long. It lives in the American deserts, resting underground in a burrow by day and coming out to feed at night.

The Gila monster feeds on eggs, nesting birds, ground squirrels, young rabbits and any other small animals that live on the ground. It can only move slowly, so it relies on ambush to catch prey. The Gila is not an aggressive lizard, but will defend itself by hissing at and then biting anything that attacks it.

It has an excrutiatingly painful bite. The lower jaw contains venom glands and when it bites, venom flows from these glands into grooves in the teeth. The lizard cannot inject poison into its prey or attacker, as a snake does, so it grips on to a victim fiercely and has to chew to work the poison in. The Gila's venom affects an animal's nervous system, so is useful for immobilizing prey. It is painful, and causes sickness and vomiting in humans, but is rarely fatal.

Mighty lizard

The Komodo dragon (below) is the largest lizard in the world. It can grow over 2m long and weighs up to 200kg. The dragon has no natural enemies on the islands where it lives, and is a fierce predator, feeding on wild boar, deer, dogs, goats, snakes, water buffalo and even humans once in a while. The Komodo dragon tends to hunt by ambush. It lumbers along forest trails, sniffing out prey with its massive, flickering, forked tongue.

The Komodo can smell animals from as far as 5km away and lies in wait for them in tall grass. Despite its clumsy appearance, the dragon can move very fast, and charges out of its hiding place once prey comes too close.

A Komodo cannot keep up a chase for long, but even if it does not manage to hang on to the prey, it sinks its teeth in to subdue it. The dragon's breath smells foul, as its mouth is full of poisonous bacteria. Even if the prey escapes, one bite is enough to cause a fatal wound. As infection sets in, the animal weakens, slows down and eventually dies. The dragon soon tracks it down again.

Moving in for the kill

The Komodo dragon's attack is ferocious and deadly. It pins its prey down on the ground with its powerful front legs and massive claws, then rips it apart. Like a shark, the dragon has bone-crushing jaws and sharp teeth with serrated edges that can tear through the toughest hide. The Komodo devours every morsel of its prey, including bones, fur and hooves, ripping off large chunks of flesh and gulping them down whole.

◄ The massive Komodo dragon has all the trademarks of a predator. Its enormous size, powerful jaws, scaly, leathery hide, giant front legs and lethal, long claws make it a truly daunting sight.

► A brightly patterned cone snail extends its proboscis towards an unwary fish. As soon as the snail makes contact, a sharp modified tooth shoots down the proboscis like a hollow dart, stabbing the fish with a powerful venom.

◄ The pufferfish puffs itself up with water and erects its spines to scare off enemies and make itself hard to eat. Some types of pufferfish are poisonous, but only if they are eaten, as their poison is concentrated in their internal body organs.

Underwater stingers

Danger lurks in unexpected places beneath the ocean waves. Many sea creatures have poisonous spines which they use to defend themselves from predators. Others, such as cone snails, use poison to catch prey. There are more than 50 different kinds of poisonous fish in the world's oceans. They make many people ill every year, and have even been known to cause death. Some of these fish are almost invisible, lying camouflaged on the sea-bed. Others have bold, colourful markings, to warn potential predators not to attack, or eat them.

Hidden danger

The stonefish is possibly the most deadly fish in the sea. It lives on corals and rocks in shallow, tropical waters and relies on ambush to catch its prey. Its squat, warty body is camouflaged with splodges of colour that make it almost invisible. The stonefish lies in wait until a small fish or crustacean comes close enough to seize, then swallows it whole.

The stonefish can hardly move and is unable to escape from predators, so it has a row of spines along its back which are tough enough to pierce sandstone. The minute the spines are touched, or someone treads on them, they release deadly venom which affects the breathing muscles and heart, causing suffocation or a heart attack.

◄ A stonefish lies concealed on the rocky seabed. It allows weeds and sea anemones to grow on its skin, to help camouflage it.

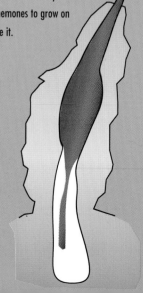

► At the base of each stonefish spine is a venom gland. When pressure is applied to the skin covering the spine, venom shoots up a canal to the sharp tip of the spine.

◄ The long spines along a lionfish's back are disguised within frond-like fins. Each spine has a venom gland lying in a long central groove. If a lionfish is threatened, it swims towards its attacker with all these dorsal spines pointing forwards, ready to attack.

But these feathery fins contain a battery of lethal poisonous spines – 13 along its back, three beneath its tail fins and two below its jaw. These spines contain poison glands, but the poison is used only for defence and never for hunting. Any predator trying to eat a lionfish is speared by the spines and is unlikely to survive. The lionfish's stripes warn predators that it is poisonous and they should keep away. A person stung by a lionfish will suffer great pain, convulsions and breathing difficulties.

▼ Sea urchins have sharp spines, but most of them are not toxic. The flower sea urchin, however, is very poisonous, and dangerous.

Deadly snail

Cone snails are tropical sea snails. Most species eat worms and other snails. A few, however, eat fish. Cone snails cannot move fast enough to chase fish, so they use poison to paralyze their prey.

The poison is delivered by means of a hollow dart. When the snail's snout touches a fish, it triggers a flow of poison. The dart in the snail's proboscis shoots out like a harpoon and injects the poison under pressure. Fish-eating cone snails are the most dangerous. They produce a nerve toxin strong enough to paralyze a fish within seconds, or to kill a person. Medical scientists are currently researching the use of cone snail venom as a non-addictive pain killer 1,000 times stronger than morphine.

Warning colours

Lionfish drift through the shallow, sunlit waters of tropical coral reefs, moving as close as they can to shoals of small fish on which they feed. Lionfish are extremely beautiful, with gauzy striped and dotted fins that they hold aloft like fluttering fans. Their stripes help to camouflage them against the background of the coral reef as they float waiting for prey.

Two of the most dangerous creatures in the sea are armed not with powerful jaws and sharp teeth, but with trailing tentacles and deadly poison. The box jellyfish is the most poisonous sea creature of all and has toxins more potent than a cobra's. A person who has been badly stung can die within five minutes. Blue-ringed octopuses are tiny, yet more people in Australia die as a result of their bites each year than die from shark bites.

When they do sting people, it is usually by accident, or just a self-defence reflex. Many jellyfish are carnivorous. The smaller ones feed on plankton, and the bigger ones on fish and crustaceans, such as shrimps.

The box jellyfish, sometimes known as the sea wasp, swims near the coasts of northern Australia and Southeast Asia. Like other jellyfish, it pulses gently through the water, trailing its tentacles. It has 60 tentacles, each 3m long.

The surface of each tentacle is packed with thousands of stinging cells called nematocysts. If hairs on these cells are triggered by contact with prey, they fire tiny barbed harpoons, injecting the prey with venom. Each nematocyst is tiny, but because there are so many of them, this can result in a huge amount of venom. One box jellyfish tentacle alone can kill an adult human.

◀ Box jellyfish have a pale blue translucent bell about 20cm across. The bell has four distinct sides, hence the name 'box jellyfish'.

▶ During the jellyfish season, huge swarms of jellyfish float out to sea, carried to and fro by the tides and currents. Moon jellyfish are common and widespread, but their stings are not powerful enough to harm humans.

▼ Each nematocyst contains poison and a tightly coiled harpoon. When the harpoon is triggered, it shoots out of the cell at great speed, turns itself inside out and sticks into the victim, releasing a shot of venom.

Once prey has been immobilized by the stings, the jellyfish lifts it to its mouth with its tentacles. On humans, box jellyfish stings cause agonizing pain and produce weal-like scars up to half a centimetre wide. As with other jellyfish, even when a box jellyfish has died and its tentacles are dry, they can still sting if they come into contact with soft, wet skin.

Small but deadly

The blue-ringed octopus is tiny but deadly. It measures only 20cm across with its tentacles outstretched, yet the venom glands in its head contain enough poison to kill ten men.

▼ The blue-ringed octopus prefers to hide or flee rather than attack. Like other octopuses, it uses jet propulsion to swim, taking water into its bag-like body, then forcing it out behind it to propel it forwards. It makes its body as streamlined as possible, to increase its speed.

The octopus lives in shallow waters and rock pools around Australia and Pacific Ocean islands, where it hunts for crabs. Its tentacles are lined with suckers, but these are harmless to humans. It is the bite from the octopus that is lethal. The octopus has sharp jaws like a parrot's beak. When it bites its prey or a person, it injects venomous saliva into the wound. The venom causes paralysis, heart failure and death.

The octopus is normally a dull yellow colour with pale blue circles, but if it is feeding, feels threatened or trapped, its body colour darkens and the circles turn electric blue, warning predators that it is poisonous. Young blue-ringed octopuses do not have the blue rings, and rely on squirting out clouds of ink to escape from predators, like other octopuses Once the blue rings have developed, however, they no longer need to do this.

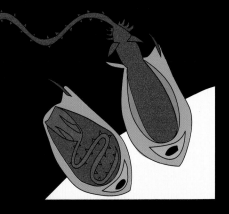

SUMMARY OF CHAPTER 2: VENOMOUS CREATURES

Venomous creatures

This chapter looked at the different ways in which animals use poison to kill their prey or defend themselves. It also looked at how poisons work. Some affect an animal's nervous system, leading to suffocation or heart attack. Others stop an animal's blood from flowing.

Deadly snakes

Poisonous snakes do not hunt people but use venom to immobilize or kill the small animals that they eat. Some snakes, such as the king cobra, have venom strong enough to kill an elephant.

Poisonous skin

Amphibians, such as frogs, toads and salamanders, have poisonous skin to discourage predators from eating them. Their bright colouring acts as a warning to their attackers.

Dangerous lizards

Two different kinds of lizard, the Gila monster and the enormous Komodo dragon, are poisonous. The Gila monster has a toxic bite which causes sickness and vomiting in humans; the Komodo dragon has a mouth full of deadly bacteria which it chews into its victims, causing a slow and very painful death.

Poisonous sea creatures

Many sea creatures use venom to catch their prey or protect themselves from attack. The stonefish and lionfish both have poisonous spines that are used purely in self-defence. Cone snails, on the other hand, are slow-moving sea snails that use a powerful poison to paralyze their prey. Jellyfish have long tentacles, armed with thousands of tiny stinging cells, that they trail through the water. The tiny blue-ringed octopus has a deadly poisonous bite, making it one of the most dangerous creatures in the sea. The venom glands in the head of the blue-ringed octopus contain enough poison to kill ten men!

Go further...

 For detailed information on animals, plus quizzes and printouts to colour in, visit:
www.enchantedlearning.com

Visit the National Aquarium of Baltimore's website for information on animals that live in the sea:
www.aqua.org

Learn more about the Gila monster at: www.gila-monster.org

The Blue Planet by Andrew Byatt, Alastair Fothergill and Martha Holmes (BBC, 2001)

The British Natural History Museum Book of Predators by Steve Parker (Carlton, 2001)

 Herpetologist
A specialist who studies reptiles and amphibians.

Zoo-keeper
Summer work experience at a zoo would help you find out about the job.

Museum work
Classifying species and preparing exhibits for display to the public.

Marine biologist
Specializes in marine ecology.

Television researcher
Does the background research for natural history television programmes.

 Visit London Zoo, one of the world's first scientific zoos, and explore the reptile house.
www.londonzoo.co.uk
London Zoo,
Regent's Park,
London, NW1 4RY
T: 020 7722 3333

The Natural History Museum is Britain's national museum of natural history. Here, you will have the opportunity to find out more about animals large and small.
www.nhm.ac.uk
The Natural History Museum,
Cromwell Road,
London, SW7 5BD
T: 020 7942 5011

CHAPTER 3

Small but deadly

When people think of dangerous creatures, the first that spring to mind are the large carnivores. Yet some of the tiniest creatures are just as frightening and even more dangerous.

Many people squirm at the thought of creepy crawlies – and the sight of a scorpion with its tail raised or a large hairy spider is enough to fill anyone with terror.

Though many scorpions and spiders are harmless, some of them are really deadly. Other small creatures have become legendary for being lethal. Piranhas are famous for tearing their victims apart in minutes, and vampire bats are linked with legends of bloodsucking monsters that roam at night. In fact, the biggest killers of all are also the smallest. The mosquito kills millions of people every year by spreading malaria. Other insects spread many nasty diseases. These insects are all tiny, yet they are responsible for far more deaths than sharks, crocodiles or snakes.

Sydney funnel web spider

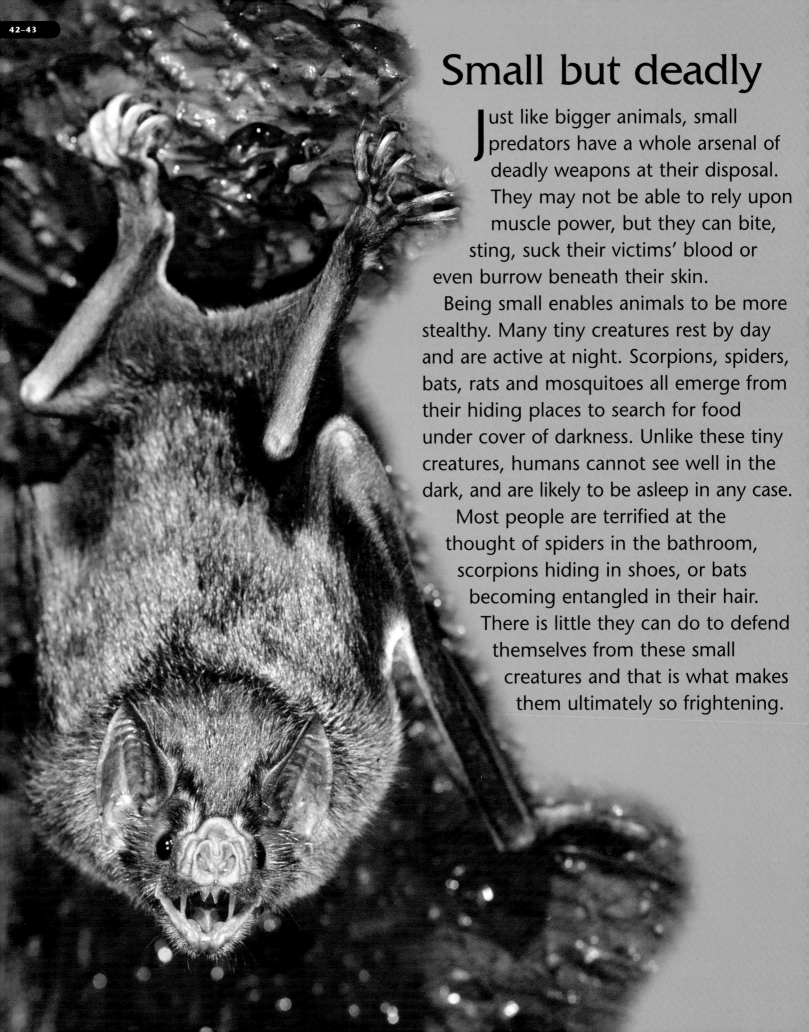

Small but deadly

Just like bigger animals, small predators have a whole arsenal of deadly weapons at their disposal. They may not be able to rely upon muscle power, but they can bite, sting, suck their victims' blood or even burrow beneath their skin.

Being small enables animals to be more stealthy. Many tiny creatures rest by day and are active at night. Scorpions, spiders, bats, rats and mosquitoes all emerge from their hiding places to search for food under cover of darkness. Unlike these tiny creatures, humans cannot see well in the dark, and are likely to be asleep in any case.

Most people are terrified at the thought of spiders in the bathroom, scorpions hiding in shoes, or bats becoming entangled in their hair. There is little they can do to defend themselves from these small creatures and that is what makes them ultimately so frightening.

Dangerous teeth

Animals do not have to be large to have a dangerous bite. Piranhas (right) are only 30cm long, yet they are armed with powerful jaws and fierce teeth. One piranha on its own may not be able to kill an animal, but a shoal of piranhas can.

Vampire bats (left) use their razor-sharp front teeth to make cuts in their victims' skin, so they can suck their blood. Rats are equipped with immensely strong teeth which can gnaw through most things.

Potent poisons

Many tiny creatures use venom to subdue or kill their prey, or to defend themselves from attack. Spiders have poisonous fangs, scorpions wield a nasty sting at the end of their tails, and bees use their venomous stings as the ultimate form of defence. In some cases, a spider's or scorpion's venom is stronger than that of a snake, which is a much bigger animal.

Spreading disease

Many insects, such as mosquitoes, tsetse flies and fleas, are not poisonous in themselves, but they kill millions of people and livestock every year by spreading infectious diseases whenever they bite.

All of these insects feed on the blood of animals or people. Once they have become infected with a disease – as a result of feeding from an infected animal or person – they pass it on to any other creature they feed from. Small as they are, these insects really are deadly, and there is little that people can do to prevent them from spreading infection.

Sinister spiders

Many people are terrified of spiders. All spiders have a poisonous bite, and they use it to subdue or kill their prey. Most of the 50,000 or so species of spider are harmless to humans, but a few are dangerous. Their bites can cause long-lasting wounds, and can even lead to death if not treated with antivenin promptly.

▲ The brown recluse spider, found in the United States, is only just over 1cm long. It looks harmless, but its venom is a lethal mixture of chemicals that destroy body tissue and cause painful ulcers which do not heal. The spider often bites people, but deaths are rare.

▼ A gigantic bird spider sinks its large fangs into a mouse. To attack, it rears up, then strikes downwards, injecting venom into its prey with fangs that are 1cm long. Bird spiders also eat young birds that they drag from their nests.

Hairy giants

Gigantic bird spiders, the biggest spiders of all, have a leg span of 28cm, so the largest are the size of dinner plates. They are found throughout South America in tropical rainforests, and hunt small animals. Bird spiders only bite people in defence, as a last resort. If they feel threatened, they release a cloud of tiny barbed hairs which work their way into a person's skin and cause severe irritation.

Black widow spiders

The black widow is considered the most venomous spider in North America, with venom that is 15 times more poisonous than that of the prairie rattlesnake. In fact, like most spiders, the black widow eats insects. The female usually hides upside-down in her web. When an insect gets caught in the web, the spider bites holes in its body and sucks out the insides. Only the female black widow is poisonous; the males and spiderlings are harmless. Yet the spider's bite is not usually fatal to humans, as it injects only a small amount of venom. Black widows have this name because of the belief that the female black widow kills and eats the male spider once she has mated. This happens only occasionally.

▶ The female black widow is shiny black in colour, with a reddish hourglass shape on the underside of her abdomen. The male is only about half her size, with a smaller body and longer legs.

Funnel web spider

The Sydney funnel web is the most dangerous spider of all. Its fangs are strong enough to drive through a fingernail, and its venom is powerful enough to kill a human unless they are treated with antivenin quickly. The spider is found in the suburbs around Sydney, and the males often come into contact with people when searching for a mate. Like bird spiders, the funnel web rears up to strike so that it can stab its fangs downwards. Its venom attacks the nervous system, paralyzing the muscles and causing severe breathing difficulties.

Cunning web

As the name suggests, the entrance to a funnel web spider's web is shaped like a funnel, and leads down into a burrow lined with spider's silk. The spider also spins long strands of silk that stretch out from the entrance of the web, like guy ropes from a tent. These strands act like tripwires. The spider hides just inside the entrance to its burrow, waiting for prey. As soon as a frog, lizard or insect trips on one of the threads, the spider feels the vibrations and rushes out of the hole to seize its victim.

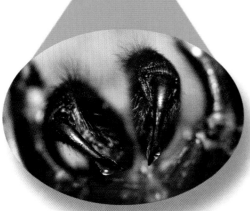

▲ The Sydney funnel web's fangs drip with venom when it is about to strike. Only 7mm long, the fangs are enormous in relation to the size of the spider's head, and are sharp enough to pierce the skull of a small animal. Only the male funnel web's venom is harmful to humans. A toxic mixture of acids and nerve poisons, it is made in venom glands behind the spider's fangs.

▶ A Sydney funnel web spider hides in its web. As soon as an insect trips on one of the tripwires, the spider attacks.

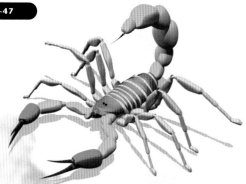

▲ When a scorpion feels threatened or is about to attack, it opens both front claws and raises its tail. A scorpion's tail is very flexible, being made up of five separate segments with a bulb-shaped part called the telson at the end.

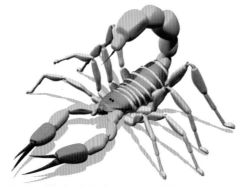

▲ If prey is difficult to hold, the scorpion carefully arches its sting forwards, right over its back, to aim at a soft spot on its victim, such as a joint. Each type of scorpion has venom that works on the animal it eats, such as insects or crustaceans.

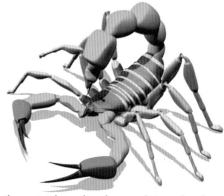

▲ The scorpion jabs its tail into the prey and injects a dose of venom. It rocks the sting to and fro to work its way into the victim's flesh. Meanwhile, muscles around the scorpion's venom glands contract, squeezing the poison through the hollow sting into the prey.

Sting in the tail

The sight of a scorpion hiding in a shoe or scuttling across a bathroom floor strikes terror into the hearts of most people. All scorpions are poisonous and, despite being small, some of them produce venom powerful enough to kill a person.

Scorpions are arachnids, so they belong to the same animal family as spiders, ticks and mites. Like other arachnids, they have jointed legs, but they also have giant pincers and a segmented tail with a poisonous sting at the tip. There are about 1,500 different types of scorpion living around the world, but only 25 of them are dangerous to humans.

Open claws show aggression

▶ At the tip of the fat-tailed scorpion's tail there is a swollen, bulb-shaped segment ending in a long, sharp, hollow spine. Inside the bulb are two venom sacs full of poison. Muscles attached to the base of the bulb move the sting backwards and forwards.

African fat-tailed scorpion

During the mating season, male scorpions often wander into houses looking for females. They find hiding places under beds and in other nooks and crannies.

Like all scorpions, the fat-tailed scorpion is a predator and hunts soft-bodied prey, such as spiders, centipedes, cockroaches, beetles and even other scorpions. It catches animals in its pincers, then stings the victim to stun it. Some scorpions have such powerful pincers that they crush their prey and do not need to sting it. Small scorpions with weak pincers, however, use their venom so they can catch prey as large as themselves.

Scorpions also use their stings to defend themselves. The fat-tailed scorpion's venom is as strong as that of a cobra, but the reason it is dangerous is that the tail is strong enough to pierce clothes and even shoes. The scorpion strikes several times, so it is able to inject large quantities of venom into its attacker. It is thought to kill 250 to 400 people a year in Tunisia, in northern Africa.

Death stalker

The scorpion with the most potent venom of all is the Palestine yellow scorpion, sometimes known as the death stalker. It does not inject much venom at a time, but the actual poison is far more powerful than that of a cobra. Found in deserts and other dry habitats in Asia, the Palestine yellow scorpion hides in small natural burrows or under stones. Its venom is a powerful cocktail of neurotoxins – poisons that affect the nervous system. Unless treated quickly with antivenin, the scorpion's sting leads to coma, convulsions and fever. The victim will usually die of heart failure or breathing difficulties.

▼ Unlike most other scorpions, the Palestine yellow scorpion has both slender claws and a narrow tail. Other scorpions have either huge claws or a fat tail.

Night prowler

Scorpions are thought of as desert animals, but in fact they are found in many other habitats as well, from grasslands to rainforests. The African fat-tailed scorpion, the most dangerous scorpion to humans, originally lived in shallow burrows or under rocks in northern Africa. As its territory has become more built up, however, it has moved into people's homes. It particularly likes damp places, such as bathrooms, where there are plenty of insects to catch.

▲ Piranhas only mount a serious attack when they are swimming in a shoal. They swim just beneath the surface of the water with all their senses alert for signs of movement or disturbance that might indicate prey.

Fierce fish

Piranhas have the reputation of being the world's fiercest fish. Terrifying stories tell of people falling into the River Amazon, in South America, and being stripped of all flesh within minutes, amidst waters boiling with angry fish. It is true that piranhas are armed with frightening jaws and sharp teeth, but of the 20 to 26 different species of piranha, only four may be dangerous to humans and then only in particular situations. In fact, no case has ever been recorded of anyone having been killed by piranhas.

Tropical home

Piranhas are found only in South America, from Venezuela down to Argentina. They live in the mighty, slow-moving rivers, such as the Amazon, that flow through the tropical rainforests into the Atlantic Ocean. Despite their reputation, piranhas have wide-ranging appetites. Most of them eat fruit and seeds, or nip bites out of the fins and scales of other fish, which soon grow back. The most dangerous of the species are the red-bellied piranhas.

▶ As with most animals, the front teeth of a fish provide vital clues to what it eats. The red-bellied piranha has powerful, deep jaws, a blunt face and a mouth full of thin, triangular teeth as sharp as knife blades. These teeth can slice through an animal's flesh easily, each bite leaving a crescent-shaped cut about the width of an adult's thumb.

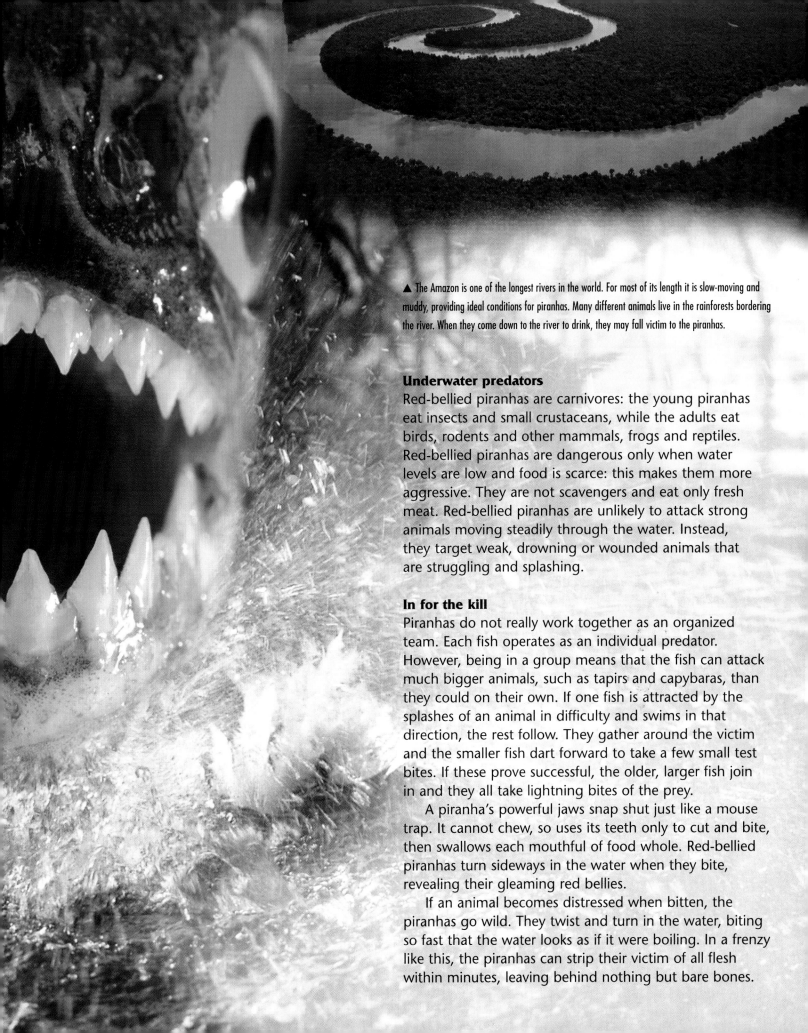

▲ The Amazon is one of the longest rivers in the world. For most of its length it is slow-moving and muddy, providing ideal conditions for piranhas. Many different animals live in the rainforests bordering the river. When they come down to the river to drink, they may fall victim to the piranhas.

Underwater predators

Red-bellied piranhas are carnivores: the young piranhas eat insects and small crustaceans, while the adults eat birds, rodents and other mammals, frogs and reptiles. Red-bellied piranhas are dangerous only when water levels are low and food is scarce: this makes them more aggressive. They are not scavengers and eat only fresh meat. Red-bellied piranhas are unlikely to attack strong animals moving steadily through the water. Instead, they target weak, drowning or wounded animals that are struggling and splashing.

In for the kill

Piranhas do not really work together as an organized team. Each fish operates as an individual predator. However, being in a group means that the fish can attack much bigger animals, such as tapirs and capybaras, than they could on their own. If one fish is attracted by the splashes of an animal in difficulty and swims in that direction, the rest follow. They gather around the victim and the smaller fish dart forward to take a few small test bites. If these prove successful, the older, larger fish join in and they all take lightning bites of the prey.

A piranha's powerful jaws snap shut just like a mouse trap. It cannot chew, so uses its teeth only to cut and bite, then swallows each mouthful of food whole. Red-bellied piranhas turn sideways in the water when they bite, revealing their gleaming red bellies.

If an animal becomes distressed when bitten, the piranhas go wild. They twist and turn in the water, biting so fast that the water looks as if it were boiling. In a frenzy like this, the piranhas can strip their victim of all flesh within minutes, leaving behind nothing but bare bones.

Killer bees

Africanized honey bees look very similar to their relatives, the well-loved European honey bees. However, they are far more aggressive and attack anyone approaching their nests, earning them the name 'killer bees'. Since arriving in South America in the 1950s, they have spread rapidly northwards into the USA, without anyone being able to halt their progress.

▼ A bee's sting is made up of two barbed darts held together in a sheath and connected to a venom gland. When the bee stings, muscles drive the darts deep into the victim's flesh.

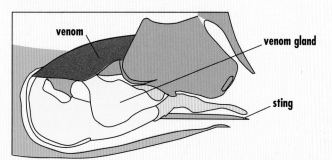

venom

venom gland

sting

Bees from Africa

Africanized honey bees, as their name implies, are not native to South America. In 1956, a professor working at a university in Brazil took 63 queen bees from Africa to Brazil. He wanted to breed a new honey bee that could produce a lot of honey in the tropical climate of Brazil – and African bees had the most productive colonies he had found. Some of the queen bees escaped and bred with local bees, creating a new type of bee: the Africanized honey bee. These bees were similar in many ways to their African ancestors. They were aggressive and quick to take over the hives of local bees. More worryingly, however, they were ferocious about defending their hives, so much so that many beekeepers gave up beekeeping altogether.

◀ Like other honey bees, killer bees feed on nectar and pollen from flowers, and produce honey from the nectar.

▶ Swarms of bees, such as this one in the eaves of a house, are less dangerous than nesting bees as they do not need to protect a hive or the growing larvae inside it.

The bees had few natural enemies in South America, so they flourished in their new environment and started spreading. By 1986, they had reached Mexico and now they have settled in the southern states of the USA as well.

Swarming bees

Like other honey bees, Africanized honey bees live in large colonies. From time to time, a colony flies away to find a new nesting site. While waiting for a scout to find a good place, the whole colony rests on a tree or house in a huge mass called a swarm. European honey bees may swarm only once a year, but Africanized honey bees form swarms six to 12 times a year.

The bees often build their nests in man-made objects, such as holes or cracks in buildings, under mobile homes, in sheds or in log piles. This brings them into close contact with people. They build smaller nests than European bees, as the climate is warmer and they do not need to store honey in their hives over the winter.

However, the bees attack and sting any person or animal that approaches their nest. Like other bees, they die as soon as they have stung something, so they sting in defence only. The bees give chase for up to half a kilometre. As each bee stings the attacker, it gives off a warning scent, calling other bees to join in the attack. Even bees from other colonies join in, so there could be thousands of bees altogether. Each bee sting is no stronger than a bee sting from another species of bee, such as the European honey bee, but the number of stings is highly dangerous and they can kill a person unless treated promptly. Since the 1950s, about 1,000 people have died from attacks by killer bee swarms.

▶ Africanized honey bees look very similar to European honey bees, but they are slightly smaller, only 2cm long.

Spreading disease

Some of the most deadly animals in the world are also the smallest. Many insects spread germs and diseases – ranging from food poisoning, a short-term illness, to real killers, such as malaria and sleeping sickness.

Most diseases are caused by bacteria, viruses or tiny single-celled creatures called protozoa. All these things are parasites, which means that they feed and breed on other animals. Parasites need a way to move from one host animal to another – and when they do so, they spread disease. Many lethal parasites are carried from one host to another by insects.

▲ The common house fly eats any food it can find, spitting on it to turn it into a soupy liquid it can mop up. The fly breeds on animal dung, rotten meat and vegetables. It can carry millions of harmful germs both on and inside its body.

▲ Screwworm maggots take a week to mature on their host animal. By this stage they look like small screws, hence their name. When they are about 15mm long, they drop off their host and form pupae on the ground. Flies emerge within three days.

▶ When a female anopheles mosquito lands on a person's skin, she points her long proboscis at it. This acts as a sheath for tiny pointed probes called stylets which sink into the skin and enable her to draw up blood.

proboscis

Body invaders
The female screwworm fly lays up to 400 eggs in open wounds on humans and other animals. The eggs hatch into larvae which burrow into the host's flesh and feast on it until they are full-size maggots. The maggots' saliva is toxic and makes smelly pus that attracts more flies to lay eggs. If the animal or person is not treated quickly, they become ill and die. In the past, millions of cattle were infected with screwworm flies, but now they have been eradicated in many areas as governments have bred sterile male flies to prevent the females laying eggs.

▲ Fleas jump between one animal or bird and another and feed by sucking their blood. Fleas can spread deadly diseases, such as typhus. The Bubonic Plague, which killed millions of people in Europe, was carried by fleas living on black rats.

▶ This tsetse fly is full of blood that it has just sucked from a human. If the fly is carrying a parasite, it can pass the deadly disease of sleeping sickness on to every person it bites. The victim will think he or she has the flu at first, but will then become very ill.

Biggest killer

Indirectly, the mosquito kills more people than any other animal, by transmitting the deadly disease malaria. There are 2,500 different species of mosquito and they carry many diseases, but only the female anopheles mosquito carries the parasite that causes malaria.

Male mosquitoes feed on nectar from plants, but female mosquitoes drink blood because they need the protein it contains to help them grow eggs. They can land on most parts of a person's body without him or her even realizing they are there. If a mosquito has already drunk blood infected with malaria, it infects more people every time it bites. This is because it injects a small amount of saliva into a person's skin when it bites, to keep the blood flowing. Although malaria can be treated, over 1 million people still die from the disease in Africa every year.

A deadly bite

The tsetse fly is part of the same family as the house fly. It is tiny, yet it is infecting half a million people living in Africa each year – 80 per cent of whom will eventually die.

The tsetse fly feeds on the blood of animals and humans. It often carries a single-cell parasite, called trypanosome, that works its way into the body and attacks the blood and nervous systems of its victims. In humans, it causes sleeping sickness – a painful disease that ends in coma and death, unless treated. Any human who is not treated for the disease then becomes a potential host for healthy flies. These flies become infected when they bite their human carrier and spread the disease even further.

In animals, the tsetse fly causes a disease called nagana. This kills 3 million livestock animals every year, leading to huge economic losses in 36 African countries, many of which are already desperately poor to start with.

Sadly, although sleeping sickness is fairly easy to treat, the medicine is very expensive. The World Health Organization estimates it costs about £19 million a year to fight the disease.

◀ Vampire bats find their way in the dark by echolocation. They make tiny sounds which bounce off objects in their flight path. The bats pick up the echoes that come back to them and use the information to pinpoint where things are.

Vampire bats

The mere name of a vampire bat conjures up nightmares. For centuries, this small, bloodsucking bat has been linked in people's minds with myths about the souls of the dead wandering through the night to suck the blood of living people. In fact, the vampire bat feeds mainly from pigs, cows and horses. The main threat to humans comes from the fact that the bat spreads disease.

▲ The common vampire has long, triangular incisors with sharp cutting edges. With these, it makes a small, wound about 3cm deep in its victim's flesh.

Bloodsucking bats

Vampire bats are found in northern Mexico and South America. They are the only bats that feed on other animals' blood. They need to consume half of their body weight in blood every night, and may die if they do not feed for two nights in a row. There are three types of vampire bat: the white-winged and hairy-legged vampire bats feed mainly from birds, but the common vampire bat feeds from mammals.

Common vampires are about the size of a mouse, with a wingspan of 30 to 35cm. They live in colonies: there are usually about 100 bats in a colony, but numbers can reach up to 2,000. The bats roost by day and search for food at night, flying about 1m above the ground, looking for herds of animals.

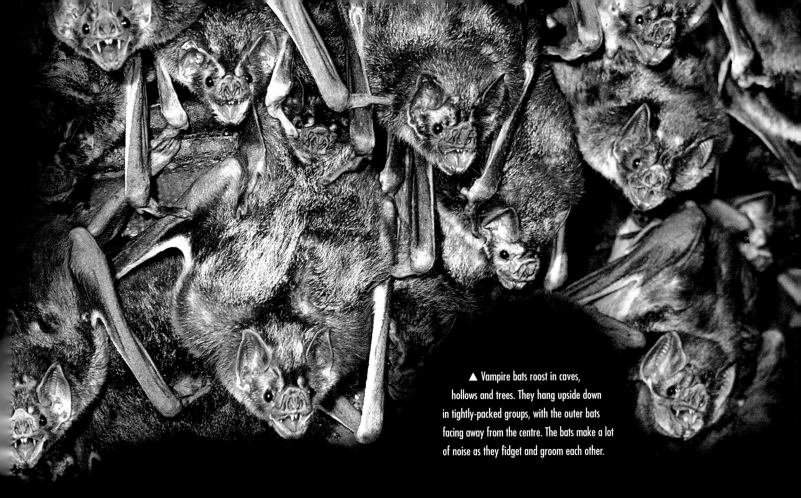

▲ Vampire bats roost in caves, hollows and trees. They hang upside down in tightly-packed groups, with the outer bats facing away from the centre. The bats make a lot of noise as they fidget and groom each other.

Stealthy techniques

Once it has found an animal, a vampire bat uses heat sensors in its nose to find a good spot to feed, such as veins close to the skin. Unlike other bats, a vampire bat can move backwards and sideways like a spider, and run and jump. This agility makes it easier for it to attach itself to prey.

The bat snips off any fur or hair with its teeth and makes a cut in the animal's skin. It then sticks its tongue into the wound and laps up the blood. The bat's saliva produces anticoagulant – a chemical that stops the animal's blood from clotting and keeps it flowing. Another chemical in the saliva numbs the animal's skin so that it does not feel anything. The bat feeds for up to 40 minutes. Then, it uses its strong back legs and thumbs to catapult itself back into the air.

Vampire bats do not harm animals by draining them of their blood, but they do spread disease, especially rabies, which kills over 200,000 cattle every year. Also, very occasionally, they feed from people, who can also die from rabies. Another problem is that the anticoagulant in bats' saliva prevents wounds from healing properly, leading to serious infection.

▼ Vampire bats bite animals in places where it is hard to shake them off. They often feed from between the ears or eyes, or on the neck, back or shoulders. Humans are bitten on the tips of their fingers and toes, their ears, their noses and even their lips.

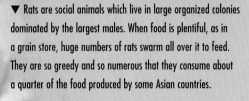

▲ Brown rats are 40 to 45cm long, including the rope-like tail. Their fur is rough and mostly brown, speckled with black on the back. Brown rats' bellies are grey or a creamy-white colour.

Rats

Rats are one of the world's worst pests. Aggressive and highly destructive, they cause widespread damage. They eat about one fifth of the world's crops every year, pollute food, destroy electric and telephone cables and damage homes and properties. They also kill livestock, such as chickens, ducks and even lambs. But most dangerous of all, they are known carriers of several diseases that can be fatal to humans.

▲ Like other rodents, rats have sharp front teeth that carry on growing throughout their lives. Rats constantly gnaw hard things, such as lead pipes and cables, to keep their teeth short and sharp.

▼ Rats are social animals which live in large organized colonies dominated by the largest males. When food is plentiful, as in a grain store, huge numbers of rats swarm all over it to feed. They are so greedy and so numerous that they consume about a quarter of the food produced by some Asian countries.

An adaptable and successful pest

The most common species of rat in Europe and North America is the brown rat, also called the Norway rat or sewer rat. It first came to Europe in the 18th century CE, brought from the East in sailing ships. Until then, the black rat reigned supreme in Europe, but the brown rat was larger and more aggressive. It drove the black rat off its territory, leaving it to live on ships and in dockland areas.

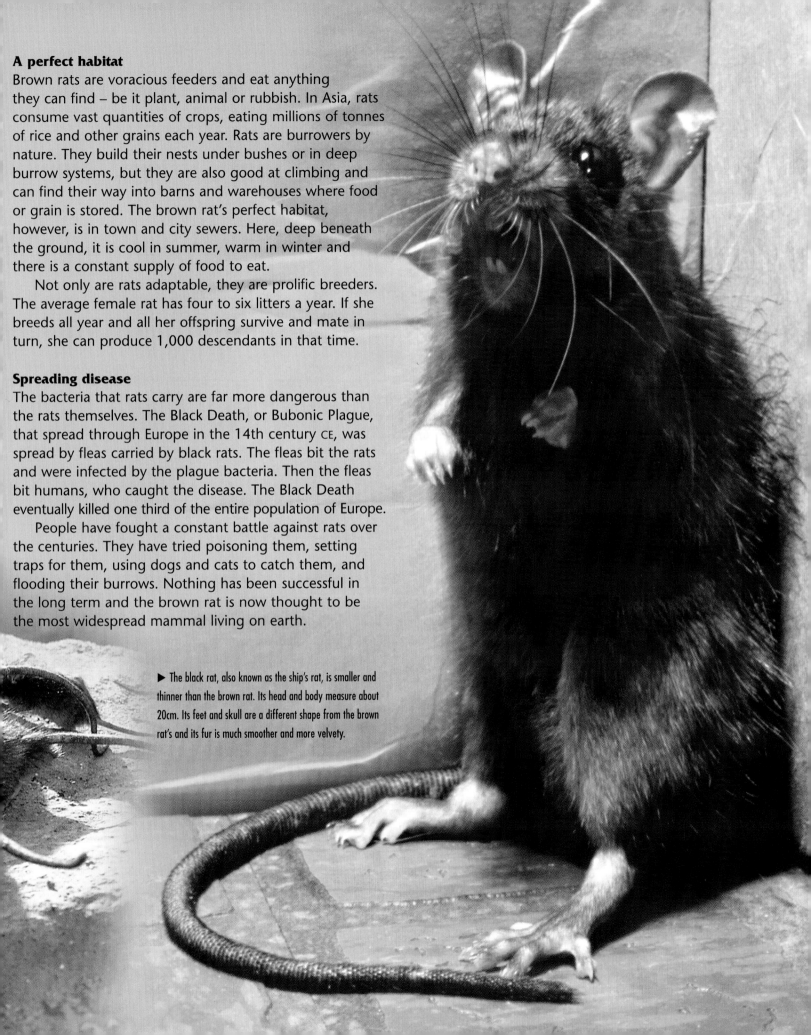

A perfect habitat

Brown rats are voracious feeders and eat anything they can find – be it plant, animal or rubbish. In Asia, rats consume vast quantities of crops, eating millions of tonnes of rice and other grains each year. Rats are burrowers by nature. They build their nests under bushes or in deep burrow systems, but they are also good at climbing and can find their way into barns and warehouses where food or grain is stored. The brown rat's perfect habitat, however, is in town and city sewers. Here, deep beneath the ground, it is cool in summer, warm in winter and there is a constant supply of food to eat.

Not only are rats adaptable, they are prolific breeders. The average female rat has four to six litters a year. If she breeds all year and all her offspring survive and mate in turn, she can produce 1,000 descendants in that time.

Spreading disease

The bacteria that rats carry are far more dangerous than the rats themselves. The Black Death, or Bubonic Plague, that spread through Europe in the 14th century CE, was spread by fleas carried by black rats. The fleas bit the rats and were infected by the plague bacteria. Then the fleas bit humans, who caught the disease. The Black Death eventually killed one third of the entire population of Europe.

People have fought a constant battle against rats over the centuries. They have tried poisoning them, setting traps for them, using dogs and cats to catch them, and flooding their burrows. Nothing has been successful in the long term and the brown rat is now thought to be the most widespread mammal living on earth.

▶ The black rat, also known as the ship's rat, is smaller and thinner than the brown rat. Its head and body measure about 20cm. Its feet and skull are a different shape from the brown rat's and its fur is much smoother and more velvety.

SUMMARY OF CHAPTER 3: SMALL BUT DEADLY

Deadly stings and fangs

This chapter looked at the ways in which the smallest creatures of all can be very dangerous – not only to the animals they hunt, but also to any humans they may come into contact with.

Scorpions use the stings at the ends of their tails to subdue prey before eating it. Some scorpions, such as the Palestine yellow scorpion, have venom as strong as or stronger than that of a cobra. Scorpions are dangerous to people only when they sting in defence, if threatened or stepped upon. Unless treated quickly, people can die from their stings.

Some spiders are even more dangerous. They have poisonous fangs which they sink into their prey, injecting enough venom to kill it. A few spiders, such as the Sydney funnel web, are armed with venom powerful enough to kill humans.

Africanized honey bees – often known as killer bees – are not predators, but they are very aggressive and will sting animals or people repeatedly if their hive is threatened. This is the ultimate self-sacrifice as, like other bees, killer bees die as a result. Each individual sting is no more powerful than that of a European honey bee, but the cumulative effect of so many stings can be fatal.

Ferocious teeth

Red-bellied piranhas are said to be the fiercest fish in the world. Despite their small size, a shoal of piranhas can strip prey clean of all flesh within minutes in a feeding frenzy. They are, however, aggressive and dangerous only when water levels are low and food is scarce.

Spreading disease

Many small creatures are dangerous because they spread disease. Mosquitoes, tsetse flies and fleas all infect people and livestock with deadly diseases. The screwworm maggot burrows beneath animals' skin and literally eats their flesh, causing horrible infections. Vampire bats (left) spread a deadly disease called rabies as they move from one animal to another, sucking their blood. Rats carry all kinds of bacteria and fleas that also carry disease.

Go further...

For an excellent website on insects, which includes information on spiders and scorpions:
www.earthlife.net/insects

Find out more about scorpions:
www.desertusa.com

Visit the National Geographic's fun site for kids to find out about vampire bats and many of the big predators:
www.nationalgeographic.com/

Nightmares of Nature by Richard Matthews (HarperCollins, 1995)

Inside Guides: Amazing Bugs by Miranda MacQuitty (Dorling Kindersley, 1996)

Entomologist
Person who specializes in the study of insects.

Ichthyologist
Someone who specializes in studying fish.

Conservationist
Someone who promotes the preservation of natural resources and the environment.

Epidemiologist
Person who studies epidemic diseases.

Visit the creepy crawlies at the Natural History Museum, Britain's national museum of natural history.
www.nhm.ac.uk
The Natural History Museum,
Cromwell Road,
London, SW7 5BD
T: 020 7942 5011

Dive into the deep and watch the sharks at the London Aquarium.
www.londonaquarium.co.uk
London Aquarium,
County Hall,
Westminster Bridge Road,
London, SE1 7PB
T: 020 7967 8000

Glossary

amphibian
An animal such as a frog, toad or salamander that spends most of its life on land but has to return to water in order to breed.

antivenin
A blood serum containing antibodies which counteract the effects of an animal venom. Antivenin is usually made from the venom it is treating.

arachnid
A member of the group of animals that includes spiders and scorpions. All arachnids have simple eyes and four pairs of legs.

bacterium (plural: bacteria)
A simple, single-celled organism which is so small that it can only be seen under a microscope. Many bacteria can cause disease.

bill
A bird's beak.

bird of prey
A bird, such as an eagle or owl, that hunts and kills other animals to eat.

blubber
A thick layer of fat just beneath a sea mammal's skin, which helps it to keep warm and survive extreme cold.

camouflage
Colouring, patterns or markings that help an animal to blend in with its surroundings, so that it is hard for either predators or prey to see it.

canine teeth
The four sharp, pointed, fang-like teeth at the front of an animal's mouth on either side of its incisors.

canopy
The part of a rainforest where the trees spread out their branches high up, like the top of an umbrella.

carcass
The dead body of an animal.

carnivore
An animal that eats mainly meat.

colony
A group of the same type of animal, such as bats, that all live together.

crustacean
An animal with a shell, such as a shrimp or crab.

digest
To soften and break food down into very small particles that the body is able to absorb.

hippopotamuses

dominance
A position of control over others established by the strongest and most powerful animal in a group.

echolocation
The way in which some animals, such as bats, find their way around by making sounds, then using the returning echoes to locate objects.

entrails
An animal's intestines, the long tube through which food passes after leaving the stomach.

environment
An animal's or person's surroundings.

fang
A long, sharp tooth.

gizzard
A bird's second stomach, in which the food that it has eaten is ground up.

gland
A body organ that produces a particular substance, such as poison.

habitat
The area where an animal lives, such as grassland, sea or rainforest.

incisors
The sharp-edged front teeth in the lower and upper jaws.

larva (plural: larvae)
An insect in the first stage of its life, after it has hatched from the egg.

maggot
The larva of certain types of fly.

mammal
An animal that gives birth to live young and feeds them on milk.

mucus
Moist, sticky slime.

musth
A period of aggressive behaviour that the males of some large animals, such as elephants, go through.

muzzle
An animal's nose and mouth.

nematocyst
A tiny stinging cell on a jellyfish, anemone or coral. When triggered, the cell shoots out a harpoon-like thread which injects venom into the prey or attacker.

paralyze
To make an animal or person unable to move.

parasite
A creature that is dependent on another living animal for its food. It cannot live apart from its host animal.

pellet
A small ball of undigested material, that some birds, such as owls, cough up after they have eaten. An owl pellet consists mostly of bones.

pincers
The enlarged claws of animals such as scorpions, that pinch together to catch and hold prey.

plankton
Microscopic plants and animals that float in the sea and lakes and form the basis of the food chains there.

pod
A small group of animals such as whales or seals.

polyp
A tiny creature that has a tube-shaped body. Coral polyps are the small creatures whose skeletons form coral reefs once the polyps die.

predator
An animal that hunts and kills other animals to eat.

prey
Animals that are hunted and killed by other animals.

pride
A family group of lions.

proboscis
The long, tube-like mouthpart of some creatures, such as cone snails and mosquitoes.

protein
A substance found in all living things, which animals need to eat in order to grow and remain healthy.

rainforest
A thick forest, with very tall trees, that grows in tropical countries where it is hot all the time and rains every day.

raptor
Another name for a bird of prey, such as an eagle or hawk.

reptile
A cold-blooded animal, such as a snake or crocodile, that often has scaly skin. Some reptiles lay eggs and others give birth to live young.

retract
To pull back in.

rodent
A small mammal, such as a rat, which has large front teeth for gnawing.

roost
A place where bats or birds rest.

great white shark

saliva
The liquid in an animal's mouth that moistens food, starts breaking it down as part of the digestive process and helps the animal to swallow.

scute
A bony plate on the back of an animal such as a crocodile, which makes its skin tougher and helps to protect it from attack.

secrete
To produce something.

sensor
A device for detecting information about physical things, such as heat, light, movement or sounds.

serrated
Having a jagged edge, like the edge of a steak knife.

sheath
A close-fitting protective cover.

shoal
A large number of fish swimming together.

snout
An animal's projecting nose.

species
A particular type of animal or plant.

talons
The long, sharp curved claws of a bird of prey.

tentacle
A long, flexible, arm-like part of the body of certain animals, such as octopuses, which is used for both movement and for grasping things.

territory
The area in which an animal lives and hunts for its food.

toxic
Poisonous, or caused by poisons.

toxin
A poisonous substance, especially one formed in the body.

translucent
Allowing some light to shine through, but not transparent or completely see-through.

tropical
To do with the tropics, parts of the world on either side of the Equator where it is usually hot.

venom
The poisonous fluid made by some animals, such as snakes, scorpions and spiders.

virus
A microscopic organism that multiplies inside the body cells of a host animal. Viruses spread easily and many of them cause diseases.

Index

Acknowledgements

The publisher would like to thank the following for permission to reproduce their material. Every care has been taken to trace copyright holders. However, if there have been unintentional omissions or failure to trace copyright holders, we apologize and will, if informed, endeavour to make corrections in any future edition.

Key: b = bottom, c = centre, l = left, r = right, t = top

1 Oxford Scientific Films (OSF); 4 Getty Images; 7 Getty Images; 8 Natural History Picture Agency (NHPA); 9 Steve Bloom; 10*tl* Getty Images; 10–11 Steve Bloom; 11*br* Steve Bloom; 12*tl* NHPA; 12*br* Steve Bloom; 13 NHPA; 14*bl* Steve Bloom; 14–15*tr* NHPA; 15*br* Getty Images; 16*tl* Nature Picture Library (Nature); 16*tr* Corbis; 16–17*cb* Steve Bloom; 17*cl* Steve Bloom; 18*bl* Still Pictures; 19*tl* Steve Bloom; 19*br* Ardea; 20*tl* NHPA; 20*b* OSF; 21*t* Getty Images; 22–23 Steve Bloom; 22*b* OSF; 23*t* Corbis; 24 NHPA; 25 Corbis; 26 Frank Lane Picture Agency; 27 Getty Images; 28*t* National Geographic Image Collection; 28*b* Corbis; 29*t* NHPA; 29*b* Corbis; 32*tl* Nature; 32–33 Getty Images; 33*t* Nature; 33*b* Nature; 34*tl* Getty Images; 34*tr* Ardea; 34–35 Ardea; 36*tl* Corbis; 36*tr* Corbis; 36*bl* Corbis; 37*c* NHPA; 37*br* Nature; 38*b* Ardea; 39*t* Frank Lane Picture Agency; 39*b* Corbis; 40 Corbis; 41 Alamy; 42 NHPA; 43 Corbis; 44*t* NHPA; 44*b* NHPA; 45*t* NHPA; 45*c* NHPA; 45*cb* OSF; 46–47 OSF; 47*br* NHPA; 48*tl* OSF; 48–49*c* Corbis; 48–49*b* OSF; 49*t* Corbis; 50*t* OSF; 51*tr* Ardea; 51*b* OSF; 52*tl* Corbis; 52*cl* Corbis; 52*bl* Corbis; 52–53 Corbis; 53*tr* Corbis; 54*t* Science Photo Library (SPL); 54*b* Ardea; 55*t* Still Pictures; 56*tl* Nature; 56*tr* Ardea; 56*b* OSF; 57 SPL; 59 Steve Bloom; 59 Corbis; 64 Steve Bloom

The publisher would like to thank the following illustrators:
10–11 cheetah skeleton/Tom Connell; 16 chimp attack diagram/Mike Davis; 23 shark attack diagram/Mike Davis; 30–31 snake heads/Jurgen Ziewe; 36 sting diagram/Mike Davis; 39 sting diagram/Mike Davis; 45 spider nest art/Mike Davis; 46 scorpion art/Mike Davis; 50 sting diagram/Mike Davis

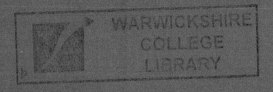